10-Minute Moments: God's Story
Growing in Your Faith Ten Minutes at a Time

Credits
Author: Kurt Johnston
Executive Developer: Nadim Najm
Chief Creative Officer: Joani Schultz
Assistant Editor: Rob Cunningham
Cover Art Director/Designer: Riley Hall
Production Manager: DeAnne Lear

ISBN 978-0-7644-6301-3

10 9 8 7 6 5 4 3 2 1   17 16 15 14 13 12 11 10 09
Printed in the United States of America.

INTRODUCTION

When I was about your age, I heard a pastor say that unless I spent at least an hour a day reading my bible and praying I wasn't a real Christian. As you can probably imagine, that was pretty confusing for me to hear. Because I didn't know much about the Bible and didn't feel too comfortable praying, I decided it was better to just not try at all than to try to spend an hour every day and fail. As a result, I hardly ever read my bible, or prayed or spent any "alone" time with God.

What I've figured out over the years is this: Spending a little bit of time with God every day is way, way, way better than not spending any time at all. I've also learned that it's almost impossible to spend a whole hour with Him and that I'm not a bad Christian just because I don't do that.

That's really the reason the "10-Minute Moment" booklets were created. I wanted to create a simple tool to help young teenagers like you spend just a little bit of time with God every day. Believe it or not, in just 10 minutes you can read a little bit from the Bible, think about what you just read and how it might apply to your life, and talk to God a little bit. Each "10-Minute Moment" booklet is written to provide you with about a month's worth of 10-minute moments with God and usually focuses on a certain topic that I think might be interesting or important for young teens.

This "10-Minute Moment" is going to take you on a short journey through the entire Bible! The whole Bible is meant to give you a look at God's story...His plan for you and me from the moment He created the world right up to today and beyond. My buddy, Josh Pease, who is super smart and knows a TON about the Bible, worked hard to make sure each 10-minute moment was going to be worth your time and would be something that helped you understand God's story a little better.

I think you will be surprised at how easy and how interesting it can be to spend 10 minutes of alone time with God. I also think you'll be surprised to discover how amazing, wonderful, and powerful God's story really is!

I'm praying for you,

Kurt Johnston

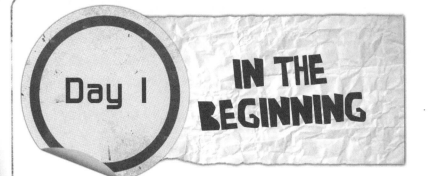

Day 1

IN THE BEGINNING

Every story has a beginning, like in those old fairly tales that start with "once upon a time." Or the classic beginning to Star Wars that starts "a long time ago, in a galaxy far, far away."

God's story has a beginning too … the difference being that His story is totally true!! In the Bible passages for today we find out that everything was created by God – including us. Which means we're pretty important! From the very beginning, God wanted us to be a part of His story.

2 MINUTES

Read the passage several times (as many times as you can in 2 minutes).

Genesis 1:1-5 (NLT)
¹In the beginning God created the heavens and the earth. ²The earth was formless and empty, and darkness covered the deep waters. And the Spirit of God was hovering over the surface of the waters.

³Then God said, "Let there be light," and there was light. ⁴And God saw that the light was good. Then he separated the light from the darkness. ⁵God called the light "day" and the darkness "night."

And evening passed and morning came, marking the first day.

Genesis 1:26-31 (NLT)
²⁶Then God said, "Let us make human beings in our image, to be like us. They will reign over the fish in the sea, the birds in the sky, the livestock, all the wild animals on the earth, and the small animals that scurry along the ground."

[27]So God created human beings in his own image. In the image of God he created them; male and female he created them.

[28]Then God blessed them and said, "Be fruitful and multiply. Fill the earth and govern it. Reign over the fish in the sea, the birds in the sky, and all the animals that scurry along the ground."

[29]Then God said, "Look! I have given you every seed-bearing plant throughout the earth and all the fruit trees for your food. [30]And I have given every green plant as food for all the wild animals, the birds in the sky, and the small animals that scurry along the ground—everything that has life." And that is what happened.

[31]Then God looked over all he had made, and he saw that it was very good! And evening passed and morning came, marking the sixth day.

5 MINUTES

Think about the following questions and how they might apply to your life.
- The very first verse of the Bible tells us that GOD created everything. He just thought it up and it appeared. Have you ever created something? How powerful must God be to create everything out of NOTHING?
- If God created us, then that means each person is valuable and special. Do you know that you are valuable and special to God? Do you treat other people like they're special to Him?
- The world God created was absolutely perfect, with no anger or pain or death or crying. But the world we know now isn't like that at all. What do you think happened?

3 MINUTES

Spend 3 minutes talking to God. Here are some things to talk to Him about today.
- Think of your favorite thing in the world that God created – maybe a mountain or the ocean or an animal. Thank Him for thinking that up and creating it for you to enjoy.

- It's only because of God that we exist at all. Ask Him to help you remember that He is there today.
- Everybody is important to God. Ask God for help knowing that YOU are important to Him, and treating other people the same way.

THOUGHTS

This space is here for you to jot down some thoughts, write out a prayer, draw a picture, or do whatever you want to help you remember your 10-minute moment.

Day 2

THINGS GO BAD

God created Adam and Eve to live in a perfect world and told them they could do whatever they wanted. The only rule was that there was one tree they couldn't eat from... other than that, the world was theirs. All they had to do was obey.

2 MINUTES

Read the passage several times (as many times as you can in 2 minutes).

Genesis 2:16-17 (NLT)
16But the Lord God warned him, "You may freely eat the fruit of every tree in the garden—17except the tree of the knowledge of good and evil. If you eat its fruit, you are sure to die."

Genesis 3:1-7 (NLT)
1The serpent was the shrewdest of all the wild animals the Lord God had made. One day he asked the woman, "Did God really say you must not eat the fruit from any of the trees in the garden?"

2"Of course we may eat fruit from the trees in the garden," the woman replied. 3"It's only the fruit from the tree in the middle of the garden that we are not allowed to eat. God said, 'You must not eat it or even touch it; if you do, you will die.'"

4"You won't die!" the serpent replied to the woman. 5"God knows that your eyes will be opened as soon as you eat it, and you will be like God, knowing both good and evil."

6The woman was convinced. She saw that the tree was beautiful and its fruit looked delicious, and she wanted the wisdom it would give

her. So she took some of the fruit and ate it. Then she gave some
her husband, who was with her, and he ate it, too. ⁷At that moment
their eyes were opened, and they suddenly felt shame at their
nakedness. So they sewed fig leaves together to cover themselves.

Genesis 3:9-10 (NLT)
⁹Then the Lord God called to the man, "Where are you?"

¹⁰He replied, "I heard you walking in the garden, so I hid. I was
afraid because I was naked."

5 MINUTES

Think about the following questions and how they might apply to
your life.
- The snake in the story is Satan – an angel who disobeyed God
  and now wants to destroy everything God created. The first
  thing the serpent does is tell Adam and Eve that God's way
  isn't the best way (v. 5). Is it sometimes hard for you to believe
  that God's way is best?
- In v. 10 Adam and Eve hide from God because they're
  embarrassed about what they did. Have you ever felt like that
  when you've done something wrong?
- Is there any area in your life now where you're not doing what
  God said, and because of that it's hard to talk to Him?

3 MINUTES

Spend 3 minutes talking to God. Here are some things to talk to Him
about today.
- The truth is that God loves us, even when we do things that
  are wrong. Spend some time thanking God for loving you no
  matter what you do.
- If there is sin (something you've done to disobey God) in your
  life right now, tell God about it and let Him know you're sorry.
- Since God forgave us for everything we've ever done through
  Jesus, thank Him for forgiving you, and ask for help to not
  believe Satan's lies.

THOUGHTS

This space is here for you to jot down some thoughts, write out a prayer, draw a picture, or do whatever you want to help you remember your 10-minute moment.

Day 3

THE BLAME GAME

When sin came into the world it messed everything up. Rather than living at peace with each other and with God, Adam and Eve immediately start tempting each other to do wrong and then refuse to take responsibility for their actions.

2 MINUTES

Read the passage several times (as many times as you can in 2 minutes).

Genesis 3:6-13 (NIV)

⁶*When the woman saw that the fruit of the tree was good for food and pleasing to the eye, and also desirable for gaining wisdom, she took some and ate it. She also gave some to her husband, who was with her, and he ate it. ⁷Then the eyes of both of them were opened, and they realized they were naked; so they sewed fig leaves together and made coverings for themselves.*

⁸*Then the man and his wife heard the sound of the LORD God as he was walking in the garden in the cool of the day, and they hid from the LORD God among the trees of the garden. ⁹But the LORD God called to the man, "Where are you?"*

¹⁰*He answered, "I heard you in the garden, and I was afraid because I was naked; so I hid."*

¹¹*And he said, "Who told you that you were naked? Have you eaten from the tree that I commanded you not to eat from?"*

¹²*The man said, "The woman you put here with me—she gave me some fruit from the tree, and I ate it."*

[13]Then the LORD God said to the woman, "What is this you have done?" The woman said, "The serpent deceived me, and I ate."

5 MINUTES

Think about the following questions and how they might apply to your life.

- According to v. 6, what does Eve do after she eats the fruit? Why do you think she does that? Why does Adam agree?
- Have you ever felt pressured into doing something that was wrong? Have you ever PUT pressure on someone to do what was wrong? Why do you think we want other people to do bad things with us?
- What do Adam and Eve do in vs. 13-14?
- Whenever you get caught doing something wrong do you normally take responsibility, or do you try to talk/excuse/blame your way out of it?

The truth is that sin always, always, always makes us feel guilty. And when we feel guilty we do one of two things – we try to get other people to do it too (so we don't feel alone in our guilt) or we pretend what we did wasn't wrong at all by blaming others or claiming "it wasn't my fault."

But if we're going to be in a good relationship with God – and that's what He wants for us – we've got to learn to be honest about our own sin.

3 MINUTES

Spend 3 minutes talking to God. Here are some things to talk to Him about today.

- Is there an area in your life where you feel pressured to do the wrong thing? Pray to God and ask Him to help you stand up for what's right.
- Is there something you're doing that you know is wrong – maybe you're getting other people to do it too (for example, gossip, lying, cheating)? Ask God to help you want to do the right thing, not the wrong thing.

• Do you blame others when you get in trouble or try to explain why what you did wasn't really wrong (even when you know it was?) Ask God to help you be the kind of person who admits when you've done wrong things.

This space is here for you to jot down some thoughts, write out a prayer, draw a picture, or do whatever you want to help you remember your 10-minute moment.

Day 4

GOD'S PLAN WHEN THINGS GO WRONG

Adam and Eve messed up. They disobeyed God and believed Satan's lies. From that point on every human would be eternally separated from God. But God wasn't okay with leaving it that way. He had a plan …

Read the passage several times (as many times as you can in 2 minutes).

Genesis 3:8-19 (NIV)

8Then the man and his wife heard the sound of the LORD God as he was walking in the garden in the cool of the day, and they hid from the LORD God among the trees of the garden. 9But the LORD God called to the man, "Where are you?"

10He answered, "I heard you in the garden, and I was afraid because I was naked; so I hid."

11And he said, "Who told you that you were naked? Have you eaten from the tree that I commanded you not to eat from?"

12The man said, "The woman you put here with me—she gave me some fruit from the tree, and I ate it."

13Then the LORD God said to the woman, "What is this you have done?" The woman said, "The serpent deceived me, and I ate."

14So the LORD God said to the serpent, "Because you have done this, "Cursed are you above all the livestock and all the wild animals! You will crawl on your belly and you will eat dust all the days of your life.

¹⁵And I will put enmity between you and the woman, and between your offspring and hers; he will crush your head, and you will strike his heel."

¹⁶To the woman he said, "I will greatly increase your pains in childbearing; with pain you will give birth to children. Your desire will be for your husband, and he will rule over you."

¹⁷To Adam he said, "Because you listened to your wife and ate from the tree about which I commanded you, 'You must not eat of it,' "Cursed is the ground because of you; through painful toil you will eat of it all the days of your life.

¹⁸It will produce thorns and thistles for you, and you will eat the plants of the field.

¹⁹By the sweat of your brow you will eat your food until you return to the ground, since from it you were taken; for dust you are and to dust you will return."

5 MINUTES

Think about the following questions and how they might apply to your life.

- You might remember that the snake in this story is Satan. In v. 15 it says that the descendants of humans and the snake (Satan) would fight. This verse says that Satan would hurt one of the humans, but that this human would destroy Satan. Who do you think this verse is talking about?
- Thousands of years after Adam and Eve, Jesus came and defeated Satan! He was who that verse was talking about! The second after the worst mistake humans ever made, God had a plan. If God had a plan then, do you think God still has a plan for your life?

3 MINUTES

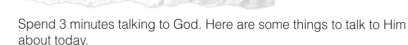

Spend 3 minutes talking to God. Here are some things to talk to Him about today.

- Thank Jesus for coming and dying for you. Thank Him that there's NOTHING you can ever do that'll make Him love you less.
- The whole mess of sin started when Adam and Eve believed Satan's lies instead of God's truth. Ask God to help you know the difference between His plan and Satan's lies.
- Tell God about the things you'll need help with today. Ask Him to use you to help other people.

THOUGHTS

This space is here for you to jot down some thoughts, write out a prayer, draw a picture, or do whatever you want to help you remember your 10-minute moment.

NOAH

If you grew up going to church (or if you've seen the movie Evan Almighty) you probably know the story of Noah, the guy God told to build an ark, then put two of every animal on it. But there's more to this story – God floods the earth and every human or animal not on the ark dies. This isn't a story for kids. It's actually a story that can be hard to understand. Why would God do such a thing?

2 MINUTES

Read the passage several times (as many times as you can in 2 minutes).

Genesis 6:5-8 (NLT)

5The Lord observed the extent of human wickedness on the earth, and he saw that everything they thought or imagined was consistently and totally evil. 6So the Lord was sorry he had ever made them and put them on the earth. It broke his heart. 7And the Lord said, "I will wipe this human race I have created from the face of the earth. Yes, and I will destroy every living thing—all the people, the large animals, the small animals that scurry along the ground, and even the birds of the sky. I am sorry I ever made them." 8But Noah found favor with the Lord.

Genesis 7:1-4 (NLT)

1When everything was ready, the Lord said to Noah, "Go into the boat with all your family, for among all the people of the earth, I can see that you alone are righteous. 2Take with you seven pairs—male and female—of each animal I have approved for eating and for sacrifice, and take one pair of each of the others. 3Also take seven pairs of every kind of bird. There must be a male and a female in each pair to ensure that all life will survive on the earth after the flood. ⁴Seven days from now I will make the rains pour down on the earth. And it will rain for forty days and forty nights, until I have wiped from the earth all the living things I have created."

Genesis 9:12-15 (NLT)
¹²Then God said, "I am giving you a sign of my covenant with you and with all living creatures, for all generations to come. ¹³I have placed my rainbow in the clouds. It is the sign of my covenant with you and with all the earth. ¹⁴When I send clouds over the earth, the rainbow will appear in the clouds, ¹⁵and I will remember my covenant with you and with all living creatures. Never again will the floodwaters destroy all life."

Think about the following questions and how they might apply to your life.

- During the creation story we read earlier, God creates man and says "it is very good." Now, a few chapters later, God says He is "sorry He even made them." What do you think happened in between (look at v. 5)? What does this tell you about how our choices make God feel?
- If God is so disappointed with humans, why do you think He takes time to save Noah, his family, and the animals?

When reading this story two things stand out about God: 1) it made Him sad to do what He had to, 2) He never gave up on His plan for humanity. The same plan God had since Adam and Eve sinned was still in place.

Spend 3 minutes talking to God. Here are some things to talk to Him about today.

- At the beginning of the story God is brokenhearted over the sins of humans. Pray that God would show you anything in your life that makes Him sad. If anything comes up, thank Jesus for forgiving you already and ask for help not to do it anymore.

• Ask God to show you what His plan is for your life today. Pray specifically for anything you're struggling with – a class, a friend, parents, anything.

TH●UGHTS

This space is here for you to jot down some thoughts, write out a prayer, draw a picture, or do whatever you want to help you remember your 10-minute moment.

ABRAHAM

As time moved on, God chose and promised a man named Abram – later renamed Abraham – to be the founder of a great nation. But the path Abraham took to see that promise come true wasn't always an easy one.

2 MINUTES

Read the passage several times (as many times as you can in 2 minutes).

Genesis 12:1-3 (NLT)
¹The Lord had said to Abram, "Leave your native country, your relatives, and your father's family, and go to the land that I will show you. ²I will make you into a great nation. I will bless you and make you famous, and you will be a blessing to others. ³I will bless those who bless you and curse those who treat you with contempt. All the families on earth will be blessed through you."

Genesis 21:1-6 (NLT)
¹The Lord kept his word and did for Sarah exactly what he had promised. ²She became pregnant, and she gave birth to a son for Abraham in his old age. This happened at just the time God had said it would. ³And Abraham named their son Isaac. ⁴Eight days after Isaac was born, Abraham circumcised him as God had commanded. ⁵Abraham was 100 years old when Isaac was born.

⁶And Sarah declared, "God has brought me laughter. All who hear about this will laugh with me.

Genesis 22:1-2 (NLT)

¹Some time later, God tested Abraham's faith. "Abraham!" God called. "Yes," he replied. "Here I am."

²"Take your son, your only son—yes, Isaac, whom you love so much—and go to the land of Moriah. Go and sacrifice him as a burnt offering on one of the mountains, which I will show you."

5 MINUTES

Think about the following questions and how they might apply to your life

- In verses 1-3 what did God ask Abram to leave behind? What did God promise him in return?
- God promises Abram that He will make Abram's descendants a "great nation." But it wasn't until Abram and Sarah were very old – and well past the age of having children – that they had their first child. What do you think that was like for them to have to wait so long? Do you think Abram ever doubted God? Have you ever doubted God?
- Abraham and Sarah's only son – Isaac – was a miracle. They KNEW he was the beginning of God's promise to make their children into a great nation. That's why it was so confusing when God asked Abraham to sacrifice Isaac. Why do you think God did that?

The truth is that while God always had a great plan for Abraham's life, He wanted Abraham to trust Him. God's plan for Abraham was first and foremost that Abraham would love God and believe He wanted what's best for Abraham.

3 MINUTES

Spend 3 minutes talking to God. Here are some things to talk to Him about today.

- What is an area of your life that you need to trust God with? Pray that God would help you trust Him in that area.
- God's plan for Abraham was so that "all the world would be blessed." In other words, part of Abraham's purpose was to

help other people. Ask God to show you who the people are in your life that He wants you to help.
- God asked Abraham to sacrifice his son as a test to see if Abraham loved God more than anything else. Are there things that are more important to you than following God? Would you be willing to give those up if you had to?

TH●UGHTS

This space is here for you to jot down some thoughts, write out a prayer, draw a picture, or do whatever you want to help you remember your 10-minute moment.

Day 7 — MOSES

Just like God promised, Abraham's descendants (called the Hebrews) became a great people – so great, that their neighbors the Egyptians became afraid of them and turned them into slaves. As the years pased it seemed like God had forgotten His promise to His people. That is, until Moses came along…

2 MINUTES

Read the passage several times (as many times as you can in 2 minutes).

Exodus 3:1-12 (NLT)

1One day Moses was tending the flock of his father-in-law, Jethro, the priest of Midian. He led the flock far into the wilderness and came to Sinai, the mountain of God. 2There the angel of the Lord appeared to him in a blazing fire from the middle of a bush. Moses stared in amazement. Though the bush was engulfed in flames, it didn't burn up. 3"This is amazing," Moses said to himself. "Why isn't that bush burning up? I must go see it."

4When the Lord saw Moses coming to take a closer look, God called to him from the middle of the bush, "Moses! Moses!"

"Here I am!" Moses replied.

5"Do not come any closer," the Lord warned. "Take off your sandals, for you are standing on holy ground. 6I am the God of your father— the God of Abraham, the God of Isaac, and the God of Jacob." When Moses heard this, he covered his face because he was afraid to look at God.

7Then the Lord told him, "I have certainly seen the oppression of my people in Egypt. I have heard their cries of distress because of their harsh slave drivers. Yes, I am aware of their suffering. 8So I have come down to rescue them from the power of the Egyptians and lead them out of Egypt into their own fertile and spacious land. It is a land flowing with milk and honey—the land where the Canaanites, Hittites, Amorites, Perizzites, Hivites, and Jebusites now live. 9Look! The cry of the people of Israel has reached me, and I have seen how harshly the Egyptians abuse them. 10Now go, for I am sending you to Pharaoh. You must lead my people Israel out of Egypt."

11But Moses protested to God, "Who am I to appear before Pharaoh? Who am I to lead the people of Israel out of Egypt?"

12God answered, "I will be with you. And this is your sign that I am the one who has sent you: When you have brought the people out of Egypt, you will worship God at this very mountain."

5 MINUTES

Think about the following questions and how they might apply to your life.
- What does God say he sees in v. 7? What does He say He'll do about it in v. 8? Even though everyone THOUGHT God forgot about the Hebrew people He always had a plan.
- God tells Moses that his job is to lead the Hebrew people out of Egypt… a HUGE job! How would you have felt if God called you to do that?
- What does Moses say in v. 11? What is God's response in v. 12? What God wants Moses to know is that it's not about his abilities… it's about GOD'S.

3 MINUTES

Spend 3 minutes talking to God. Here are some things to talk to Him about today.
- God saw the suffering of the Hebrew people, just like He sees things today that He hates. Pray that God would show you the things in the world that bother Him, and that He would teach you to care about them too.

24

- Pray that God would help you see things around you today that He wants you to be a part of changing.
- Pray that God would give you the courage to do the right thing, even when it's scary.

THOUGHTS

This space is here for you to jot down some thoughts, write out a prayer, draw a picture, or do whatever you want to help you remember your 10-minute moment.

THE 10 COMMANDMENTS

After Moses led the Hebrew people out of Egypt, God formed a special relationship with them. If the Hebrew people obeyed and worshipped God, He would bless them. So that they would know how to do that, God gave them a group of rules. The most famous of these are called "The 10 commandments."

2 MINUTES

Read the passage several times (as many times as you can in 2 minutes).

Exodus 20:1-17 (NLT)

¹Then God gave the people all these instructions:

²"I am the Lord your God, who rescued you from the land of Egypt, the place of your slavery.

³"You must not have any other god but me.

⁴"You must not make for yourself an idol of any kind or an image of anything in the heavens or on the earth or in the sea. ⁵You must not bow down to them or worship them, for I, the Lord your God, am a jealous God who will not tolerate your affection for any other gods. I lay the sins of the parents upon their children; the entire family is affected—even children in the third and fourth generations of those who reject me. ⁶But I lavish unfailing love for a thousand generations on those who love me and obey my commands.

⁷ You must not misuse the name of the Lord your God. The Lord will not let you go unpunished if you misuse his name.

[8]"Remember to observe the Sabbath day by keeping it holy. [9]You have six days each week for your ordinary work, [10]but the seventh day is a Sabbath day of rest dedicated to the Lord your God. On that day no one in your household may do any work. This includes you, your sons and daughters, your male and female servants, your livestock, and any foreigners living among you. [11]For in six days the Lord made the heavens, the earth, the sea, and everything in them; but on the seventh day he rested. That is why the Lord blessed the Sabbath day and set it apart as holy.

[12]"Honor your father and mother. Then you will live a long, full life in the land the Lord your God is giving you.

[13]"You must not murder.

[14]"You must not commit adultery.

[15] You must not steal.

[16]"You must not testify falsely against your neighbor.

[17]"You must not covet your neighbor's house. You must not covet your neighbor's wife, male or female servant, ox or donkey, or anything else that belongs to your neighbor."

5 MINUTES

Think about the following questions and how they might apply to your life.

- Of all these rules, what one seems the weirdest? Why do you think God gave them that rule?
- Which one of these rules is the hardest for you to keep?
- Do you think it's possible for anyone to obey ALL of these rules ALL the time? If not, was it unfair for God to ask people to obey them?

The truth is that God gave these rules for two reasons – one reason was so they could know how He wanted them to act. The other reason was so that they would recognize they couldn't obey all the rules on their own ... that they needed God's help. It's the same way today – if we try really hard to follow all the rules we'll just feel like a failure. God wants us to depend on Him to help us.

3 MINUTES

Spend 3 minutes talking to God. Here are some things to talk to Him about today.

- Pray for an area of your life where you feel like you're always "breaking the rules." Ask God for help in doing what's right.
- If you always feel guilty or that you're "letting God down" thank Him for sending Jesus and for ALWAYS forgiving you. God wants you to love Him… not always feel like a failure.
- Are you trying to live a "good life" on your own strength? If so it may be important to recognize that you can't do it alone… that you need God's help.
- Ask God to help you show His love to other people.

THOUGHTS

This space is here for you to jot down some thoughts, write out a prayer, draw a picture, or do whatever you want to help you remember your 10-minute moment.

Day 9

JOSHUA AND THE BATTLE OF JERICHO

After years of leading God's people (the Hebrews, or Israelites), Moses died and a man named Joshua was put in charge. Joshua was scared to lead God's people – but God told Joshua He would always be with Joshua and not to be afraid. And then God gave Joshua some strange instructions…

2 MINUTES

Read the passage several times (as many times as you can in 2 minutes).

Joshua 6:2-5 (NLT)
²But the Lord said to Joshua, "I have given you Jericho, its king, and all its strong warriors. ³You and your fighting men should march around the town once a day for six days. ⁴Seven priests will walk ahead of the Ark, each carrying a ram's horn. On the seventh day you are to march around the town seven times, with the priests blowing the horns. ⁵When you hear the priests give one long blast on the rams' horns, have all the people shout as loud as they can. Then the walls of the town will collapse, and the people can charge straight into the town."

Joshua 6:20 (NLT)
When the people heard the sound of the rams' horns, they shouted as loud as they could. Suddenly, the walls of Jericho collapsed, and the Israelites charged straight into the town and captured it.

5 MINUTES

Think about the following questions and how they might apply to your life
- What is strange about God's instructions on how to defeat the city of Jericho? How is it different from how MOST armies would fight against a city?
- How do you think Joshua and the Israelites felt while marching around the city? Do you think people made fun of them?
- Have you ever felt like God wanted YOU to do something that seemed weird? It probably wasn't as crazy as marching around a city and blowing trumpets, but sometimes little things are just as scary. What are the things that make it hard to obey Him?

Joshua had to feel a little silly marching his army around a city and then blowing some trumpets and yelling really loud, right? But he did what God said, and as a result the walls of Jericho fell down. Sometimes God's instructions for us seem weird, but our job is trust that God's plan for us is best.

3 MINUTES

Spend 3 minutes talking to God. Here are some things to talk to Him about today.
- Is there a tough situation you're facing where doing the right thing is hard? If so, pray that God would give you the strength to trust Him and do what's right.
- Sometimes it's hard to obey God, because we can't see Him or hear Him. Ask God to help you remember today that He's with you.
- Spend time talking to God about any other prayer requests you might have, for you or other people.

THOUGHTS

This space is here for you to jot down some thoughts, write out a prayer, draw a picture, or do whatever you want to help you remember your 10-minute moment.

Day 10 SAMSON

After many battles with other countries, God's chosen people – the Israelites – finally had a land to call their own. But they quickly forgot about the agreement they'd made with God – to trust and obey Him. One of the big things Israelites weren't supposed to do was marry women from other nations who didn't believe in God. But they could't seem to figure out that God's plans are for a reason so they kept breaking this rule. As a result, they kept being taken captive by other nations (this happened over and over again). When this would happen God would send people – called judges – to rescue them. These judges were SUPPOSED to be examples of following God's rules. But for some judges, like Samson, it didn't always work out that way…

2 MINUTES

Read the passage several times (as many times as you can in 2 minutes).

Judges 16:4-6 (NLT)

⁴Some time later Samson fell in love with a woman named Delilah, who lived in the valley of Sorek. ⁵The rulers of the Philistines went to her and said, "Entice Samson to tell you what makes him so strong and how he can be overpowered and tied up securely. Then each of us will give you 1,100 pieces of silver."

⁶So Delilah said to Samson, "Please tell me what makes you so strong and what it would take to tie you up securely."

Judges 16:15-21 (NLT)

¹⁵Then Delilah pouted, "How can you tell me, 'I love you,' when you don't share your secrets with me? You've made fun of me three times *now, and you still haven't told me what makes you so strong!" ¹⁶She* *tormented him with her nagging day after day until he was sick to death of it.*

¹⁷Finally, Samson shared his secret with her. "My hair has never been cut," he confessed, "for I was dedicated to God as a Nazirite from birth. If my head were shaved, my strength would leave me, and I would become as weak as anyone else."

¹⁸Delilah realized he had finally told her the truth, so she sent for the Philistine rulers. "Come back one more time," she said, "for he has finally told me his secret." So the Philistine rulers returned with the money in their hands. ¹⁹Delilah lulled Samson to sleep with his head in her lap, and then she called in a man to shave off the seven locks of his hair. In this way she began to bring him down, and his strength left him.

²⁰Then she cried out, "Samson! The Philistines have come to capture you!"

When he woke up, he thought, "I will do as before and shake myself free." But he didn't realize the Lord had left him.

²¹So the Philistines captured him and gouged out his eyes. They took him to Gaza, where he was bound with bronze chains and forced to grind grain in the prison.

5 MINUTES

Think about the following questions and how they might apply to your life
- Why do you think God told the Israelite people not to marry people who didn't believe in Him?
- Why do you think Samson chose to do it anyway?
- What do you think God's best plan is for you, as you begin to think about having a boyfriend or girlfriend?

Samson thought he could do whatever he wanted, but not following God's rules got him into huge trouble.

3 MINUTES

Spend 3 minutes talking to God. Here are some things to talk to Him about today.

- Are you "going out" or "boyfriend and girlfriend" with someone right now? Ask God to help you make sure that it is the kind of relationship you should be in.
- Samson let himself be influenced by people who didn't love God. Are there people in your life like that who are influencing you? Ask God for help in 1) finding friends who love Him and 2) being a good friend to those who aren't encouraging you to do what's right, without being influenced by them.
- Thank God for wanting what's best for you, and ask Him to show you how you can live your life for Him today.

THOUGHTS

This space is here for you to jot down some thoughts, write out a prayer, draw a picture, or do whatever you want to help you remember your 10-minute moment.

Day 11

DAVID AND GOLIATH

A long time after Samson, Israel went from having "judges" to having "kings." The most famous of these kings was a guy named David. But before David became king he fought a giant named Goliath… and he was only a teenager at the time!

2 MINUTES

Read the passage several times (as many times as you can in 2 minutes).

1 Samuel 17:1-8 (NLT)

¹The Philistines now mustered their army for battle and camped between Socoh in Judah and Azekah at Ephes-dammim. ²Saul countered by gathering his Israelite troops near the valley of Elah. ³So the Philistines and Israelites faced each other on opposite hills, with the valley between them.

⁴Then Goliath, a Philistine champion from Gath, came out of the Philistine ranks to face the forces of Israel. He was over nine feet tall! ⁵He wore a bronze helmet, and his bronze coat of mail weighed 125 pounds. ⁶He also wore bronze leg armor, and he carried a bronze javelin on his shoulder. ⁷The shaft of his spear was as heavy and thick as a weaver's beam, tipped with an iron spearhead that weighed 15 pounds. His armor bearer walked ahead of him carrying a shield.

⁸Goliath stood and shouted a taunt across to the Israelites. "Why are you all coming out to fight?" he called. "I am the Philistine champion, but you are only the servants of Saul. Choose one man to come down here and fight me!

1 Samuel 17:22-23 (NLT)

²²David left his things with the keeper of supplies and hurried out to the ranks to greet his brothers. ²³As he was talking with them, Goliath, the Philistine champion from Gath, came out from the Philistine ranks. Then David heard him shout his usual taunt to the army of Israel.

1 Samuel 17:32 (NLT)

"Don't worry about this Philistine," David told Saul. "I'll go fight him!"

1 Samuel 17:48-49 (NLT)

⁴⁸As Goliath moved closer to attack, David quickly ran out to meet him. ⁴⁹Reaching into his shepherd's bag and taking out a stone, he hurled it with his sling and hit the Philistine in the forehead. The stone sank in, and Goliath stumbled and fell face down on the ground.

5 MINUTES

Think about the following questions and how they might apply to your life.

- David was just a kid around a bunch of adults, but he was the only one who was willing to fight Goliath. Have you ever been afraid to do what's right because no one else was?
- The odds were WAY against David winning against Goliath, but he won because of God's help. It says in the Bible that "if God is for us, who can be against us." What is something you would do for God if you KNEW there was no way you'd fail?
- God doesn't always guarantee we won't fail, but He DOES love it when we do crazy things, for Him, in His power. What is one way you can "face a giant" in your life this week?

The cool thing about David is that his great-great-great-great (bunch more great) grandson was Jesus. God's plan to help all the humans after the Garden of Eden was to create a people through Abraham, that would become a nation with a king, that would eventually give way to Jesus – the God/man who would save us ALL. Of course David didn't know all this. We don't always know the big stuff God wants to use us for…

3 MINUTES

Spend 3 minutes talking to God. Here are some things to talk to Him about today.

- The truth is God has a HUGE plan for your life. Ask God to be getting you ready for His plan for your life. You might not even know what that IS yet but that's okay… God knows.
- Ask God if there's something exciting – and maybe a little bit scary – that He wants you to do at school or at home or at church.
- Let God know you love Him, and thank Him for loving you and having a plan for your life.

THOUGHTS

This space is here for you to jot down some thoughts, write out a prayer, draw a picture, or do whatever you want to help you remember your 10-minute moment.

SOLOMON ASKS FOR WISDOM

When King David died his son, Solomon, became King of Israel. One night God appeared to Solomon in a dream and said he could ask for anything he wanted…

2 MINUTES

Read the passage several times (as many times as you can in 2 minutes).

1 Kings 3:5-14 (NLT)

⁵That night the Lord appeared to Solomon in a dream, and God said, "What do you want? Ask, and I will give it to you!"

⁶Solomon replied, "You showed faithful love to your servant my father, David, because he was honest and true and faithful to you. And you have continued your faithful love to him today by giving him a son to sit on his throne.

⁷"Now, O Lord my God, you have made me king instead of my father, David, but I am like a little child who doesn't know his way around. ⁸And here I am in the midst of your own chosen people, a nation so great and numerous they cannot be counted! ⁹Give me an understanding heart so that I can govern your people well and know the difference between right and wrong. For who by himself is able to govern this great people of yours?"

¹⁰The Lord was pleased that Solomon had asked for wisdom. ¹¹So God replied, "Because you have asked for wisdom in governing my people with justice and have not asked for a long life or wealth or the death of your enemies—¹²I will give you what you asked for! I will give you a wise and understanding heart such as no one else has had or ever will have! ¹³And I will also give you what you did not ask for—riches and fame! No other king in all the world will be compared to you for the rest of your life! ¹⁴And if you follow me and obey my decrees and my commands as your father, David, did, I will give you a long life."

5 MINUTES

Think about the following questions and how they might apply to your life.

- If God appeared to you and told you to ask for anything you wanted, what would you ask for? (Be honest!)
- Why do you think God was so happy with Solomon's choice? What could Solomon have asked for? Why was asking for wisdom better?

The truth is that if God has a plan for our life, the best gift we can get is understanding a little bit about what that plan is. That's why Solomon's request was so great!

3 MINUTES

Spend 3 minutes talking to God. Here are some things to talk to Him about today.

- Just like God gave wisdom to Solomon, He will give it to you, too. He may not make you permanently smart like He did for Solomon, but He will give you the wisdom you need to tackle the stuff you face every day. Pray that God would do that for you.
- Who is one person in your life that you think maybe needs to know God loves them? How can God use you sometime soon to help them? Pray that God would give you wisdom to know how to do that.
- Pick one thing in your life you're thankful for and tell God how much you love that He gave you that one thing.

THOUGHTS

This space is here for you to jot down some thoughts, write out a prayer, draw a picture, or do whatever you want to help you remember your 10-minute moment.

ESTHER SAVES THE JEWS

Many years after David and Solomon, Israel disobeyed God and was invaded by a foreign country (man, you would think they would learn by now wouldn't you!). All the Jews (the people of Israel… I know, they've had a lot of names right?!) were taken away from their homeland and surrounded by people who worshipped completely different gods. One day, a guy in power decided he was going to try and kill all the Jews. Remember, the Jews were God's special people – Abraham's descendants, a part of God's promise to save the world! But, as always, God had a plan – a Jewish girl named Esther who had just become queen. But Esther's plan was dangerous for her – she'd have to come into the king's presence without being invited, which could lead to her execution…

2 MINUTES

Read the passage several times (as many times as you can in 2 minutes).

Esther 4:10-14 (NLT)

10Then Esther told Hathach to go back and relay this message to Mordecai: 11"All the king's officials and even the people in the provinces know that anyone who appears before the king in his inner court without being invited is doomed to die unless the king holds out his gold scepter. And the king has not called for me to come to him for thirty days." 12So Hathach gave Esther's message to Mordecai.

13Mordecai sent this reply to Esther: "Don't think for a moment that because you're in the palace you will escape when all other Jews are killed. 14If you keep quiet at a time like this, deliverance and relief for the Jews will arise from some other place, but you and your relatives will die. Who knows if perhaps you were made queen for just such a time as this?"

5 MINUTES

Think about the following questions and how they might apply to your life.

- Mordecai (Esther's uncle) tells Esther that if she doesn't take a risk God will save the Jewish people some other way. In other words, God doesn't NEED Esther, but He wants to USE her. Have you ever thought about it this way – that God doesn't NEED you to do what He wants, but that He likes using you? How does that make you feel?
- Mordecai tells Esther that maybe God has made her queen "for such a time as this." In other words, it's no accident she became queen right when the Jews needed help. What are some places God's placed you in life? At home? At school? At church? With your friends? Have you ever thought that maybe God placed you there for a reason? What do you think that might be?

3 MINUTES

Spend 3 minutes talking to God. Here are some things to talk to Him about today.

- Think about one area of your life – it could be at home, or school, an activity or sport or a friendship. Ask God why He placed that one thing in your life, and how you can use it to be part of His plan.
- Esther had a scary choice – she could have died when she went to see the king. Ultimately, though, she put aside what SHE wanted so she could do something great for God. What is one area you need that kind of courage today? Ask God to help you!
- Pray for a member of your family today, and ask God to help you show them His love through your actions.

THOUGHTS

This space is here for you to jot down some thoughts, write out a prayer, draw a picture, or do whatever you want to help you remember your 10-minute moment.

SHADRACH, MESHACH AND ABEDNEGO

Many, many years after Esther, Israel fell under the rule of the Babylonian Empire. These guys – led by King Nebuchadnezzar (neb-u-ka-nez-er) – took all the brightest, best-looking teenagers out of their homeland, and hauled them off to a foreign country to be trained under HIS rules, customs, and religion. Among this group were three guys named Shadrach, Meshach, and Abednego (Not sure why they didn't have easier names back then…like Fred, Mike, and George!). These three young men believed and worshipped the one true God in a land where no one else did. This became a problem when King Nebuchadnezzar built a massive statue of himself and demanded everyone bow down and worship it. The penalty for not doing this was to be thrown into an enormous fire.

2 MINUTES

Read the passage several times (as many times as you can in 2 minutes).

Daniel 3:8-25 (NLT)

8But some of the astrologers went to the king and informed on the Jews. 9They said to King Nebuchadnezzar, "Long live the king! 10You issued a decree requiring all the people to bow down and worship the gold statue when they hear the sound of the horn, flute, zither, lyre, harp, pipes, and other musical instruments. 11That decree also states that those who refuse to obey must be thrown into a blazing furnace. 12But there are some Jews—Shadrach, Meshach, and Abednego—whom you have put in charge of the province of Babylon. They pay no attention to you, Your Majesty. They refuse to serve your gods and do not worship the gold statue you have set up."

[13]Then Nebuchadnezzar flew into a rage and ordered that Shadrach, Meshach, and Abednego be brought before him. When they were brought in, [14]Nebuchadnezzar said to them, "Is it true, Shadrach, Meshach, and Abednego, that you refuse to serve my gods or to worship the gold statue I have set up? [15] I will give you one more chance to bow down and worship the statue I have made when you hear the sound of the musical instruments. But if you refuse, you will be thrown immediately into the blazing furnace. And then what god will be able to rescue you from my power?"

[16]Shadrach, Meshach, and Abednego replied, "O Nebuchadnezzar, we do not need to defend ourselves before you. [17]If we are thrown into the blazing furnace, the God whom we serve is able to save us. He will rescue us from your power, Your Majesty. [18]But even if he doesn't, we want to make it clear to you, Your Majesty, that we will never serve your gods or worship the gold statue you have set up."

[19]Nebuchadnezzar was so furious with Shadrach, Meshach, and Abednego that his face became distorted with rage. He commanded that the furnace be heated seven times hotter than usual. [20]Then he ordered some of the strongest men of his army to bind Shadrach, Meshach, and Abednego and throw them into the blazing furnace. [21]So they tied them up and threw them into the furnace, fully dressed in their pants, turbans, robes, and other garments. [22]And because the king, in his anger, had demanded such a hot fire in the furnace, the flames killed the soldiers as they threw the three men in. [23]So Shadrach, Meshach, and Abednego, securely tied, fell into the roaring flames.

[24]But suddenly, Nebuchadnezzar jumped up in amazement and exclaimed to his advisers, "Didn't we tie up three men and throw them into the furnace?"

"Yes, Your Majesty, we certainly did," they replied.

[25]"Look!" Nebuchadnezzar shouted. "I see four men, unbound, walking around in the fire unharmed! And the fourth looks like a god!"

5 MINUTES

Think about the following questions and how they might apply to your life

- You've probably never had a king threaten to throw you into a fire, but you probably HAVE had a situation where EVERYONE was doing something you knew you shouldn't. Is it hard to do what's right in those situations? Why? What do we get so afraid of?
- How did they respond to the king in v. 17? Do you have a relationship with God where you KNOW that whatever happens, He'll take care of you?

3 MINUTES

Spend 3 minutes talking to God. Here are some things to talk to Him about today.

- God doesn't want you to just be someone who follows the rules; He wants you to be someone that KNOWS Him, kind of like how you know a parent or a good friend. Spend just a minute today talking to Him in a way that seems normal to you. Remember, you don't have to impress Him, or say all the right things. He loves you (and already knows what you're REALLY thinking anyway!).
- What is one area in your life where you're having a hard time doing what's right? Ask God to help you with that area. Thank Him for loving you.

THOUGHTS

This space is here for you to jot down some thoughts, write out a prayer, draw a picture, or do whatever you want to help you remember your 10-minute moment.

JONAH AND THE WHALE

A long time after Shadrach, Meshach, and Abednego, the Jewish people got to move back into their home country! They were still ruled by a foreign king, but this guy mostly left them alone. During this time God told a "prophet" (which is kind of like a preacher) named Jonah to go be a missionary to the giant city of Nineveh. But Jonah HATED the people of Nineveh (mostly because they were really, really bad people) and, instead of obeying God, got on a boat going in the opposite direction. But Jonah found out that when God has a plan, there's no getting away from it.

2 MINUTES

Read the passage several times (as many times as you can in 2 minutes).

Jonah 1:1-3 (NLT)
¹The Lord gave this message to Jonah son of Amittai: ²"Get up and go to the great city of Nineveh. Announce my judgment against it because I have seen how wicked its people are."

³But Jonah got up and went in the opposite direction to get away from the Lord. He went down to the port of Joppa, where he found a ship leaving for Tarshish. He bought a ticket and went on board, hoping to escape from the Lord by sailing to Tarshish.

Jonah 1:9-12 (NLT)
⁹Jonah answered, "I am a Hebrew, and I worship the Lord, the God of heaven, who made the sea and the land."

¹⁰The sailors were terrified when they heard this, for he had already told them he was running away from the Lord. "Oh, why did you do it?" they groaned. *¹¹And since the storm was getting worse all the time, they asked him, "What should we do to you to stop this storm?"*

¹²"Throw me into the sea," Jonah said, "and it will become calm again. I know that this terrible storm is all my fault."

Jonah 1:15-17 (NLT)
¹⁵Then the sailors picked Jonah up and threw him into the raging sea, and the storm stopped at once! ¹⁶The sailors were awestruck by the Lord's great power, and they offered him a sacrifice and vowed to serve him.

¹⁷Now the Lord had arranged for a great fish to swallow Jonah. And Jonah was inside the fish for three days and three nights.

Jonah 2:1 (NLT)
Then Jonah prayed to the Lord his God from inside the fish.

Jonah 2:10 (NLT)
Then the Lord ordered the fish to spit Jonah out onto the beach.

Jonah 3:1-2 (NLT)
¹Then the Lord spoke to Jonah a second time: ²"Get up and go to the great city of Nineveh, and deliver the message I have given you."

Jonah 3:5 (NLT)
The people of Nineveh believed God's message, and from the greatest to the least, they declared a fast and put on burlap to show their sorrow.

5 MINUTES

Think about the following questions and how they might apply to your life.
- Why do you think God wanted Jonah to go to Nineveh? (Look at Jonah 3:5 for a clue.)
- God ALWAYS has a plan for us. His plan for Jonah was to use him to tell Nineveh they needed to get right with God. Do you think God has a plan for YOU to do something amazing like that?

- Even when Jonah was being disobedient, God took care of him. Can you think of a time where God has taken care of YOU, even when you were being disobedient?

3 MINUTES

Spend 3 minutes talking to God. Here are some things to talk to Him about today.
- Thank God for always taking care of you, even when you haven't always done the right thing.
- It's possible God has a super-amazing plan for your life, like He did for Jonah's. Ask God to show you what His plan for your life is. He may show you a little bit of it today, or He may show you it a month or a year from now. Keep asking!

THOUGHTS

This space is here for you to jot down some thoughts, write out a prayer, draw a picture, or do whatever you want to help you remember your 10-minute moment.

Day 16

ALMOST HERE

After Jonah, there are several other prophets God uses to speak to the Israelite people. Usually, the message God has for them is that they need to focus on LOVING Him, not just pretending to by doing the right things. And then, in the last book of the Old Testament named Malachi (another prophet), God says these words:

2 MINUTES

Read the passage several times (as many times as you can in 2 minutes).

Malachi 3:1 (NLT)
"Look! I am sending my messenger, and he will prepare the way before me. Then the Lord you are seeking will suddenly come to his Temple. The messenger of the covenant, whom you look for so eagerly, is surely coming," says the Lord of Heaven's Armies.

5 MINUTES

Think about the following questions and how they might apply to your life.
- This is a REALLY weird verse! When it says "the Lord you are seeking is suddenly coming to His temple" what does that mean? It sounds like God is saying He's coming down to man. How do you think God plans on doing that?
- There's another really weird phrase that says "the messenger of the covenant … is coming." The covenant here is a promise God made with people. Can you think of any promises we've talked about? (Look back at day 4 and day 6.)

What's happening here is that God's telling everyone that Jesus is going to be coming soon! God's way of dealing with the sin of Adam and Eve is almost here! The Jewish people didn't know all of this just yet. But looking back we can see that God's plan through ALL the stories we have read was leading to this.

That being said, after the book of Malachi God stops talking to Israel for 400 years... 400 YEARS! The Jewish people must have thought God abandoned them, but they didn't know what was about to come...

3 MINUTES

Spend 3 minutes talking to God. Here are some things to talk to Him about today.

- Thank God for how He's always in charge! All through the Old Testament He had a plan, and He does for YOUR life today too! I know we've talked about God's "plan" a whole lot, but that's the theme of His story... that He has a plan for His creation!
- Have you ever felt like God was far away or wasn't talking to you? Maybe you feel that way now. Tell God (even if He doesn't seem to be listening) that you know He's there and has a plan for your life. Tell Him you'll trust Him, even when that's really hard to do. Ask Him for help in doing that and to not be silent for long.

THOUGHTS

This space is here for you to jot down some thoughts, write out a prayer, draw a picture, or do whatever you want to help you remember your 10-minute moment.

Four-hundred years of God not talking to Israel. Imagine how alone they must have felt. Imagine how some people would have given up on believing in God altogether. But then, just when all hope seemed lost, a girl who'd never had sex gets pregnant, and angels appear to shepherds, and in the middle of the night when no one was really watching … God invaded earth. Remember that this was God's plan from the VERY BEGINNING. Thousands of years have gone by, and God has been getting things ready for the perfect time to become a human and save the world. God's plan became flesh and lived with us.

2 MINUTES

Read the passage several times (as many times as you can in 2 minutes).

Luke 2:1-15 (NLT)

¹At that time the Roman emperor, Augustus, decreed that a census should be taken throughout the Roman Empire. ²(This was the first census taken when Quirinius was governor of Syria.) ³All returned to their own ancestral towns to register for this census. ⁴And because Joseph was a descendant of King David, he had to go to Bethlehem in Judea, David's ancient home. He traveled there from the village of Nazareth in Galilee. ⁵He took with him Mary, his fiancée, who was now obviously pregnant.

⁶And while they were there, the time came for her baby to be born. ⁷She gave birth to her first child, a son. She wrapped him snugly in strips of cloth and laid him in a manger, because there was no lodging available for them.

8That night there were shepherds staying in the fields nearby, guarding their flocks of sheep. 9Suddenly, an angel of the Lord appeared among them, and the radiance of the Lord's glory surrounded them. They were terrified, 10but the angel reassured them. "Don't be afraid!" he said. "I bring you good news that will bring great joy to all people. 11The Savior—yes, the Messiah, the Lord—has been born today in Bethlehem, the city of David! 12And you will recognize him by this sign: You will find a baby wrapped snugly in strips of cloth, lying in a manger."

13Suddenly, the angel was joined by a vast host of others—the armies of heaven—praising God and saying,

14"Glory to God in highest heaven, and peace on earth to those with whom God is pleased."

15When the angels had returned to heaven, the shepherds said to each other, "Let's go to Bethlehem! Let's see this thing that has happened, which the Lord has told us about."

5 MINUTES

Think about the following questions and how they might apply to your life.

- Why do you think the angels came to shepherds with the great news about Jesus? Why didn't they go to kings, or famous people? Shepherds were as unimportant as it got – why them?
- Jesus could have been born in a royal court. He could have been a king! Instead he was born to a poor, frightened teenage girl that almost no one knew. Why do you think Jesus chose to come that way?
- A lot of times we get really wrapped up in wanting more money, attention, popularity, etc. What does this Scripture about Jesus' birth tell us? Did Jesus think these things were important?
- How did the shepherds respond when the angels told them the good news? Why do you think it was easier for THEM to be more excited about Jesus than we are? How can we work on that?

3 MINUTES

Spend 3 minutes talking to God. Here are some things to talk to Him about today.

- Thank God that He became a human – one of us – to save us from all the bad stuff we have done.
- Ask God to help you to care about the same stuff He does. Ask Him to show you if you are too concerned with money, or popularity, or success.
- Spend some time talking to Jesus about whatever's on your mind – things you are happy about, worried about, angry about, whatever! Remember, He was a human too so He knows what it is like.

TH●UGHTS

This space is here for you to jot down some thoughts, write out a prayer, draw a picture, or do whatever you want to help you remember your 10-minute moment.

Day 18 — TEMPTATION

One of the coolest things about Jesus – who was God, but man too – is that He knows what it's like to be human. Jesus had to sleep, eat, and go to the bathroom. He had to bathe or He'd be smelly. He had stinky feet from walking on a dirt road in sandals. Jesus was as much human as He was God. And this meant that – just like us – He was tempted to disobey God's rules.

2 MINUTES

Read the passage several times (as many times as you can in 2 minutes).

Luke 4:1-13 (NLT)

1Then Jesus, full of the Holy Spirit, returned from the Jordan River. He was led by the Spirit in the wilderness, 2where he was tempted by the devil for forty days. Jesus ate nothing all that time and became very hungry.

3Then the devil said to him, "If you are the Son of God, tell this stone to become a loaf of bread."

4But Jesus told him, "No! The Scriptures say, 'People do not live by bread alone.'"

5Then the devil took him up and revealed to him all the kingdoms of the world in a moment of time. 6"I will give you the glory of these kingdoms and authority over them," the devil said, "because they are mine to give to anyone I please. 7I will give it all to you if you will worship me."

8Jesus replied, "The Scriptures say, 'You must worship the Lord your God and serve only him.'"

[9]Then the devil took him to Jerusalem, to the highest point of the Temple, and said, "If you are the Son of God, jump off! [10]For the Scriptures say, 'He will order his angels to protect and guard you.

[11]And they will hold you up with their hands so you won't even hurt your foot on a stone.'"

[12]Jesus responded, "The Scriptures also say, 'You must not test the Lord your God.'"

[13]When the devil had finished tempting Jesus, he left him until the next opportunity came.

5 MINUTES

Think about the following questions and how they might apply to your life.
- What is the devil's first temptation in v. 3?
- Why do you think this one is first? Why would Jesus have been tempted by this?
- The devil claims in vs. 5-7 that he'll give Jesus all the kingdoms of the world if He'll just bow down and worship Satan. Satan was offering to make Jesus famous and powerful. How was this different from the life Jesus CAME to live?
- Have you ever been so tempted to do something that you felt there was no way to resist? How did Jesus resist Satan? (Look at vs. 4, 8,& 12.)
- Have you ever felt guilty for wanting to do wrong things? Has this ever made you feel like you can't talk to God? How does it change things knowing that Jesus was tempted too?

3 MINUTES

Spend 3 minutes talking to God. Here are some things to talk to Him about today.
- Thank Jesus for becoming a human and ultimately dying for you.
- Tell Jesus about some of the things you're struggling with. Remember, He knows what it's like to be tempted.
- Ask for God's power over those areas in your life.

TH🟠UGHTS

This space is here for you to jot down some thoughts, write out a prayer, draw a picture, or do whatever you want to help you remember your 10-minute moment.

Day 19

JESUS FIRST SERMON

We talked before about how Jesus was God's plan from the beginning. The entire Bible has been leading up to Him. As a matter of fact, throughout the Old Testament (everything before Matthew) God left clues that someone was coming to make things the way they were supposed to be. And so it's no accident when Jesus got ready to give His first sermon, He used one of these Old Testament passages to tell people that He WAS God's promise.

TWO MINUTES

Read the passage several times (as many times as you can in 2 minutes).

Luke 4:14-21 (NLT)

14Then Jesus returned to Galilee, filled with the Holy Spirit's power. Reports about him spread quickly through the whole region. 15He taught regularly in their synagogues and was praised by everyone.

16When he came to the village of Nazareth, his boyhood home, he went as usual to the synagogue on the Sabbath and stood up to read the Scriptures. 17 he scroll of Isaiah the prophet was handed to him. He unrolled the scroll and found the place where this was written:

18"The Spirit of the Lord is upon me, for he has anointed me to bring Good News to the poor. He has sent me to proclaim that captives will be released, that the blind will see, that the oppressed will be set free, 19and that the time of the Lord's favor has come."

²⁰He rolled up the scroll, handed it back to the attendant, and sat down. All eyes in the synagogue looked at him intently. ²¹Then he began to speak to them. "The Scripture you've just heard has been fulfilled this very day!"

5 MINUTES

Think about the following questions and how they might apply to your life.

- Look through vs. 18-19. Make a list of the kind of people Jesus said He had come to help.
- When Jesus says He's come to "proclaim freedom for the prisoners," what kind of prisoners do you think He means? Is He talking about people in jail for breaking the law? "If not, what other kind of prisoners are there? (Think about the story of Adam and Eve disobeying – how we have ALL been "prisoners" since then.)"
- Through the Bible, God seems to have a special passion for the poor and the sick. Why do you think that is? What do you think that means for us?

3 MINUTES

Spend 3 minutes talking to God. Here are some things to talk to Him about today.

- Thank Jesus for coming to set you free from the prison of sin.
- Ask Jesus to help you realize that you're free. Specifically pray for any area you are struggling with, and pray that Jesus' power would help you be different.
- Pray for things you, your family, or friends need. As you pray, remember that Jesus CAME to help people in need.

THOUGHTS

This space is here for you to jot down some thoughts, write out a prayer, draw a picture, or do whatever you want to help you remember your 10-minute moment.

JESUS CALLS THE FIRST DISCIPLES

Part of Jesus' plan while on earth was to surround Himself with a group of followers that He would spend practically every second with. These followers – called disciples – would one day spread the message of Jesus around the world. You're probably thinking that Jesus would have picked the smartest, most successful people to help Him…

2 MINUTES

Read the passage several times (as many times as you can in 2 minutes).

Matthew 4:18-22 (NLT)

18One day as Jesus was walking along the shore of the Sea of Galilee, he saw two brothers—Simon, also called Peter, and Andrew—throwing a net into the water, for they fished for a living. 19Jesus called out to them, "Come, follow me, and I will show you how to fish for people!" 20And they left their nets at once and followed him.

21A little farther up the shore he saw two other brothers, James and John, sitting in a boat with their father, Zebedee, repairing their nets. And he called them to come, too. 22They immediately followed him, leaving the boat and their father behind.

5 MINUTES

Think about the following questions and how they might apply to your life.
- What career did Peter, Andrew, James, and John have?
- What did they all do whenever Jesus called them?
- Does that seem weird to you that someone says "Hey, come follow me!" and they just drop everything they're doing and follow Him?

Jesus is described in the Bible as being a "rabbi" – someone who was really famous and important people in Jewish culture. To be a rabbi's follower, you'd have to be SUPER smart, and SUPER well-educated. Only the best of the best got to be a rabbi's disciple. But Jesus went to ordinary fisherman – people who were told a long time ago "you're not good enough" – and said, basically, "I think you have what it takes. I believe in you. Come follow me."

3 MINUTES

Spend 3 minutes talking to God. Here are some things to talk to Him about today.
- Did you know that the Bible says that we didn't just choose to be Christians, but that Jesus chose us too? How cool! Jesus believes in you! Thank Jesus for calling you to be His disciple.
- A disciple would spend every moment watching his rabbi, learning how he did things. Ask Jesus to help you to walk with Him every second. Ask God to change your heart and mind to care about what He cares about.
- Pray for things you, your family, or friends need. As you pray, remember that Jesus chose you, believes in you, and loves you.

THOUGHTS

This space is here for you to jot down some thoughts, write out a prayer, draw a picture, or do whatever you want to help you remember your 10-minute moment.

JESUS CALMS THE SEA

The longer Jesus was on earth, the more apparent it became that He was not a normal human, or even just a prophet of God. People began to believe that maybe Jesus really WAS the promised one God had hinted was coming – the one who would undo what happened way back in the Garden of Eden. Jesus' power wasn't just over sickness; He even seemed to have God's power to bring creation under His control. When people saw miracles like the one in this Bible passage, many began to believe.

2 MINUTES

Read the passage several times (as many times as you can in 2 minutes).

Mark 4:35-41 (NLT)

35As evening came, Jesus said to his disciples, "Let's cross to the other side of the lake." 36So they took Jesus in the boat and started out, leaving the crowds behind (although other boats followed). 37But soon a fierce storm came up. High waves were breaking into the boat, and it began to fill with water.

38Jesus was sleeping at the back of the boat with his head on a cushion. The disciples woke him up, shouting, "Teacher, don't you care that we're going to drown?"

39When Jesus woke up, he rebuked the wind and said to the waves, "Silence! Be still!" Suddenly the wind stopped, and there was a great calm. 40Then he asked them, "Why are you afraid? Do you still have no faith?"

41The disciples were absolutely terrified. "Who is this man?" they asked each other. "Even the wind and waves obey him!"

5 MINUTES

Think about the following questions and how they might apply to your life.

- Imagine you're with the disciples that night. These guys are used to being out on the sea, but this storm is so bad even THEY are freaking out. How would you be feeling?
- Does Jesus seem a little mean to you in this passage? Why does Jesus get mad at them? Does He expect us to NEVER feel afraid?
- Read v. 38. In this verse the disciples have gone beyond fear. They're now asking Jesus if He even cares about them at all. Do you think THAT'S what Jesus gets onto them about?
- Have you ever been in a really hard or painful situation where God seemed to be asleep? How did that make you feel? What can you learn from this story?

Sometimes when we feel afraid, it feels like God isn't around and we panic. The point of this story isn't don't FEEL fear. The point is don't let fear blind you to the fact that God loves and is right there with you.

3 MINUTES

Spend 3 minutes talking to God. Here are some things to talk to Him about today.

- Does God feel far away or like He doesn't care right now? If so, tell Him about how you feel. Ask Him to help you trust that He loves you.
- Is there fear in your life right now, like over grades, friends, family, sports, or the future? Give that fear to God. Ask Him to help you remember that just like He is in charge of the sea, He's also in charge of your life.
- Pray for things you, your family, or friends need. As you pray, remember that Jesus loves you, and is always close by (even when He feels far away).

THOUGHTS

This space is here for you to jot down some thoughts, write out a prayer, draw a picture, or do whatever you want to help you remember your 10-minute moment.

Day 22

JESUS DEATH

The disciples thought they had God's plan all figured out. They thought Jesus would be with them forever, and that more and more people would believe in Him. But this wasn't God's plan. What those around Jesus didn't get was that Adam and Eve's sin all those years earlier (and the sin of every person since then) had created a gap between God and man. Humans would never be in a right relationship with God unless the price for man's sins was paid – death. Jesus died in our place so that we wouldn't have to spend life on earth, and then all of eternity, separated from God.

2 MINUTES

Read the passage several times (as many times as you can in 2 minutes).

Matthew 27:27-35 (NLT)

27Some of the governor's soldiers took Jesus into their headquarters and called out the entire regiment. 28They stripped him and put a scarlet robe on him. 29They wove thorn branches into a crown and put it on his head, and they placed a reed stick in his right hand as a scepter. Then they knelt before him in mockery and taunted, "Hail! King of the Jews!" 30And they spit on him and grabbed the stick and struck him on the head with it. 31When they were finally tired of mocking him, they took off the robe and put his own clothes on him again. Then they led him away to be crucified.

32Along the way, they came across a man named Simon, who was from Cyrene, and the soldiers forced him to carry Jesus' cross. 33And they went out to a place called Golgotha (which means "Place of the Skull"). 34The soldiers gave him wine mixed with bitter gall, but when he had tasted it, he refused to drink it.

³⁵After they had nailed him to the cross, the soldiers gambled for his clothes by throwing dice.

Matthew 27:45-54 (NLT)

⁴⁵At noon, darkness fell across the whole land until three o'clock. ⁴⁶At about three o'clock, Jesus called out with a loud voice, "Eli, Eli, lema sabachthani?" which means "My God, my God, why have you abandoned me?"

⁴⁷Some of the bystanders misunderstood and thought he was calling for the prophet Elijah. ⁴⁸One of them ran and filled a sponge with sour wine, holding it up to him on a reed stick so he could drink. ⁴⁹But the rest said, "Wait! Let's see whether Elijah comes to save him."

⁵⁰Then Jesus shouted out again, and he released his spirit. ⁵¹At that moment the curtain in the sanctuary of the Temple was torn in two, from top to bottom. The earth shook, rocks split apart, ⁵²and tombs opened. The bodies of many godly men and women who had died were raised from the dead. ⁵³They left the cemetery after Jesus' resurrection, went into the holy city of Jerusalem, and appeared to many people.

⁵⁴The Roman officer and the other soldiers at the crucifixion were terrified by the earthquake and all that had happened. They said, "This man truly was the Son of God!"

5 MINUTES

Think about the following questions and how they might apply to your life.
- Why do you think Jesus had to die?
- Imagine you are one of the disciples. What would you be feeling?
- This whole scene would have been horrible to anyone watching. It would have seemed like God was a thousand miles away. But God was using ALL of this as part of His plan. Have you ever wondered why God lets hurtful things happen in your life? How do these verses help you understand why?

3 MINUTES

Spend 3 minutes talking to God. Here are some things to talk to Him about today.

- Jesus died for every human in the world, but He also died specifically for you. If you'd been the only person to exist, He would have died for you. Jesus is with you, right now as you're reading this. Talk to Him. Thank Him. Ask Him to help you know that He is with you every second of the day.

THOUGHTS

This space is here for you to jot down some thoughts, write out a prayer, draw a picture, or do whatever you want to help you remember your 10-minute moment.

ALIVE

For three days Jesus' body was dead. For three days the disciples hid in fear, thinking the same people who killed Jesus would come for them next. For three days it seemed like Jesus' message – being made right with God, hope for the hopeless, that He was the fulfillment of God's plan to save the world – was all lies.

But then, on the third day, the next phase of God's plan happened...

2 MINUTES

Read the passage several times (as many times as you can in 2 minutes).

Matthew 28:1-7 (NLT)

¹Early on Sunday morning, as the new day was dawning, Mary Magdalene and the other Mary went out to visit the tomb.

²Suddenly there was a great earthquake! For an angel of the Lord came down from heaven, rolled aside the stone, and sat on it. ³His face shone like lightning, and his clothing was as white as snow. ⁴The guards shook with fear when they saw him, and they fell into a dead faint.

⁵Then the angel spoke to the women. "Don't be afraid!" he said. "I know you are looking for Jesus, who was crucified. ⁶He isn't here! He is risen from the dead, just as he said would happen. Come, see where his body was lying. ⁷And now, go quickly and tell his disciples that he has risen from the dead, and he is going ahead of you to Galilee. You will see him there. Remember what I have told you."

Matthew 28:16 (NLT)

Then the eleven disciples left for Galilee, going to the mountain where Jesus had told them to go.

5 MINUTES

Think about the following questions and how they might apply to your life.

- Why do you think the fact that Jesus rose again is important? How would it be different if He hadn't been resurrected?
- Some people had a hard time believing Jesus really rose again. Why do you think it was hard for them to believe? Is it hard for YOU to believe?

3 MINUTES

Spend 3 minutes talking to God. Here are some things to talk to Him about today.

- One of the coolest parts about being a Christian is that we don't pray to a dead god. Mohammed, the founder of Islam, died. Buddha, the founder of Buddhism, died. Joseph Smith, the founder of Mormonism, died. Christianity is the only religion that says its founder rose again! Pray to Jesus today and thank Him for being more powerful that death.
- If God was more powerful that death, then He's definitely more powerful than anything in our life. Whatever you're struggling with, ask God to help you, using the same power He used to raise Jesus from the grave (because in the Bible it says that's exactly what He does!).

THOUGHTS

This space is here for you to jot down some thoughts, write out a prayer, draw a picture, or do whatever you want to help you remember your 10-minute moment.

Day 24

JESUS FORGIVES PETER

After Jesus was arrested but before He died, Peter told people three times He didn't even know who Jesus was. He denied Jesus because He was scared something would happen to Him too. So the first time that Peter and Jesus get a chance to talk after Jesus rose again, Jesus brings the subject up…

2 MINUTES

Read the passage several times (as many times as you can in 2 minutes).

John 21:12-19 (NLT)

12 "Now come and have some breakfast!" Jesus said. None of the disciples dared to ask him, "Who are you?" They knew it was the Lord. 13 Then Jesus served them the bread and the fish. 14 This was the third time Jesus had appeared to his disciples since he had been raised from the dead.

15 After breakfast Jesus asked Simon Peter, "Simon son of John, do you love me more than these?"

"Yes, Lord," Peter replied, "you know I love you."

"Then feed my lambs," Jesus told him.

16 Jesus repeated the question: "Simon son of John, do you love me?"

"Yes, Lord," Peter said, "you know I love you."

"Then take care of my sheep," Jesus said.

[17]*A third time he asked him, "Simon son of John, do you love me?"*

Peter was hurt that Jesus asked the question a third time. He said, "Lord, you know everything. You know that I love you."

Jesus said, "Then feed my sheep.

[18]*"I tell you the truth, when you were young, you were able to do as you liked; you dressed yourself and went wherever you wanted to go. But when you are old, you will stretch out your hands, and others will dress you and take you where you don't want to go."* [19]*Jesus said this to let him know by what kind of death he would glorify God. Then Jesus told him, "Follow me."*

5 MINUTES

Think about the following questions and how they might apply to your life.

- Why do you think Jesus asked Peter three times if he loved Him?
- In v. 17, Peter tells Jesus "You know everything…" which is true. If that's the case, why do you think Jesus asks Peter a question He already knows the answer to?

The Bible says that when Jesus died for us, He forgave everything we ever have done or ever will do. All we need to do is accept the forgiveness that He offers. When Jesus was talking to Peter, He had already forgiven Peter for what he'd done. The problem was that 1) Peter hadn't talked to Jesus about it yet and 2) Peter was feeling so guilty that he might have thought God could never use him to do ANYTHING.

But God still had big plans for Peter. The fact that Christianity exists today is partly because of how God used Peter in the years after Jesus left earth. Peter had to know God's forgiveness so that God could use Him.

3 MINUTES

Spend 3 minutes talking to God. Here are some things to talk to Him about today.

- Is there anything in your life that you know is sin, but that you haven't talked to God about? Spend some time confessing anything you need to.
- Is there any part of you that thinks God's mad at you, or that He could never use you? If so, spend some time asking God to help you understand His love. Ask Him for help with accepting His forgiveness.

THOUGHTS

This space is here for you to jot down some thoughts, write out a prayer, draw a picture, or do whatever you want to help you remember your 10-minute moment.

Day 25

JESUS LAST WORDS

After rising from the dead, Jesus showed Himself to hundreds of people, proving that He really WAS God. But He didn't stay on earth very long. God's plan – a plan still going on today – was to make it the responsibility of the followers of Jesus to tell the world His story.

And that's why Jesus' last words before going back to heaven were an explanation of what we're supposed to do...

2 MINUTES

Read the passage several times (as many times as you can in 2 minutes).

Acts 1:7-10 (NLT)
7He replied, "The Father alone has the authority to set those dates and times, and they are not for you to know. 8But you will receive power when the Holy Spirit comes upon you. And you will be my witnesses, telling people about me everywhere—in Jerusalem, throughout Judea, in Samaria, and to the ends of the earth."

9After saying this, he was taken up into a cloud while they were watching, and they could no longer see him. 10As they strained to see him rising into heaven, two white-robed men suddenly stood among them.

5 MINUTES

Think about the following questions and how they might apply to your life.
* In v. 8, what are the places Jesus tells the disciples to go?

- Those places were areas around where the disciples lived, each one farther out than the one before. What do you think this means for you? List places Jesus would want you to take the story of what He did (start close, then move farther away).
- What promise do the angels give in v. 10?

3 MINUTES

Spend 3 minutes talking to God. Here are some things to talk to Him about today.

- Jesus' last words on earth were to tell us to go and tell people about Him. Ask God to show you where you can tell people about Him. Ask Him to make you brave and loving as you do this.
- Jesus said He'd come back again for us. Talk to Him and let Him know how you feel about that. Would you WANT Him to come back tomorrow or does that make you feel nervous? Are you excited about Jesus coming back? Whatever it is, tell Him.

THOUGHTS

This space is here for you to jot down some thoughts, write out a prayer, draw a picture, or do whatever you want to help you remember your 10-minute moment.

Day 26

THE HOLY SPIRIT

Before Jesus died and rose again, He told His disciples that He would send them the Holy Spirit. The name "Holy Spirit" sounds a little weird, but Christians believe the Holy Spirit is part of the Trinity, which means that there is one God who always exists as three separate parts (it's okay if that last sentence makes your brain hurt – no one really understands it fully). What's important to know is that the Holy Spirit is God's power and presence, connected to our lives. Anyone who becomes a Christian "receives the Holy Spirit," which means that we don't do ANYTHING without having God right there with us, encouraging, supporting, convicting, and empowering us. Pretty cool, huh? And God tells us that this power is always working inside us…

2 MINUTES

Read the passage several times (as many times as you can in 2 minutes).

Romans 8:11 (NLT)
The Spirit of God, who raised Jesus from the dead, lives in you. And just as God raised Christ Jesus from the dead, he will give life to your mortal bodies by this same Spirit living within you.

5 MINUTES

Think about the following questions and how they might apply to your life.
- Spend a couple minutes rewriting what you think this verse means in your own words.

- God says that the same power that raised Jesus from the dead is at work in us. What do you think that means?

3 MINUTES

Spend 3 minutes talking to God. Here are some things to talk to Him about today.

- When Jesus left earth, He didn't leave us alone. The Holy Spirit lives inside of us now. It might seem a little weird, but pray to the Holy Spirit – the one who is working inside you. If there's anything inside of you that you know needs to change, ask for His help.
- Thank God for giving you the power to live the life you're supposed to. As you pray for your friends or family, remember that He is working through you to do something great. You are a part of His plan!

THOUGHTS

This space is here for you to jot down some thoughts, write out a prayer, draw a picture, or do whatever you want to help you remember your 10-minute moment.

THE CHURCH

After Jesus left, the disciples began their work of telling everyone about Him. As they did this, people began to believe and lives started changing. And that's how the Church first came into being. Now most people, when they think of "church," think of a building with walls and crosses and stained-glass windows. But the Church is people – anyone who believes in Jesus is a part of the Church. It's about relationships with each other and a common plan to reach the world. Look at the following verses, and the different things the Church was doing...

TWO MINUTES

Read the passage several times (as many times as you can in 2 minutes).

Acts 2:42-47 (NLT)

42All the believers devoted themselves to the apostles' teaching, and to fellowship, and to sharing in meals (including the Lord's Supper), and to prayer.

43A deep sense of awe came over them all, and the apostles performed many miraculous signs and wonders. 44And all the believers met together in one place and shared everything they had. 45They sold their property and possessions and shared the money with those in need. 46They worshiped together at the Temple each day, met in homes for the Lord's Supper, and shared their meals with great joy and generosity—47all the while praising God and enjoying the goodwill of all the people. And each day the Lord added to their fellowship those who were being saved.

5 MINUTES

Think about the following questions and how they might apply to your life.

- There's a bunch of stuff in the verse. List all the things it says the believers were doing.
- Look at your list. Is church as you experience it like this list, or not? What's different? What's the same?
- For you, is church more about a place you GO, or do you have a group of friends that you can BE the Church with?

3 MINUTES

Spend 3 minutes talking to God. Here are some things to talk to Him about today.

- God wants us to be sharing our lives with other Christians – to have close friendships that encourage and support us. THAT'S what church is. Do you have anything like that in your life? If not, pray that God would surround you with close Christian friends your age that you can BE the Church with.
- The early church we just read about was always helping the world around them. Pray that God would show you ways that you can help the people around you.

THOUGHTS

This space is here for you to jot down some thoughts, write out a prayer, draw a picture, or do whatever you want to help you remember your 10-minute moment.

As the church continued to grow, some of the disciples moved farther and farther out, telling more people about Jesus. God's plan to undo what happened in the garden of Eden through Jesus was moving fast! One of these disciples was a guy named Philip...

2 MINUTES

Read the passage several times (as many times as you can in 2 minutes).

Acts 8:26-40 (NLT)

26As for Philip, an angel of the Lord said to him, "Go south down the desert road that runs from Jerusalem to Gaza." 27So he started out, and he met the treasurer of Ethiopia, a eunuch of great authority under the Kandake, the queen of Ethiopia. The eunuch had gone to Jerusalem to worship, 28and he was now returning. Seated in his carriage, he was reading aloud from the book of the prophet Isaiah.

29The Holy Spirit said to Philip, "Go over and walk along beside the carriage."

30Philip ran over and heard the man reading from the prophet Isaiah. Philip asked, "Do you understand what you are reading?"

31The man replied, "How can I, unless someone instructs me?" And he urged Philip to come up into the carriage and sit with him.

32The passage of Scripture he had been reading was this:

"He was led like a sheep to the slaughter. And as a lamb is silent before the shearers, he did not open his mouth. 33He was humiliated and received no justice. Who can speak of his descendants? For his life was taken from the earth."

³⁴The eunuch asked Philip, "Tell me, was the prophet talking about himself or someone else?" ³⁵So beginning with this same Scripture, Philip told him the Good News about Jesus.

³⁶As they rode along, they came to some water, and the eunuch said, "Look! There's some water! Why can't I be baptized?" ³⁸He ordered the carriage to stop, and they went down into the water, and Philip baptized him.

³⁹When they came up out of the water, the Spirit of the Lord snatched Philip away. The eunuch never saw him again but went on his way rejoicing. ⁴⁰Meanwhile, Philip found himself farther north at the town of Azotus. He preached the Good News there and in every town along the way until he came to Caesarea.

5 MINUTES

Think about the following questions and how they might apply to your life.

- In v. 29 the Bible says "the Holy Spirit spoke to Philip." Since we've already said that anyone who is a follower of Jesus has the Holy Spirit living with them, do you think the Holy Spirit speaks to you too?
- Philip was able to explain to the Ethiopian how a passage of Scripture was talking about Jesus. How can you learn more about the Bible so you can explain it to people? Who's someone you could talk to who could help you with that?
- After Philip left the Ethiopian, where did he go and what did he do? Based on this, what do you think was the most important thing in Philip's life?

3 MINUTES

Spend 3 minutes talking to God. Here are some things to talk to Him about today.

- Like we said a couple days ago, the last job Jesus gave us was to tell others about Him. Pray for one person in your life that you know needs Jesus. Ask God to show Himself to this person, to open their heart to who He is. Ask the Holy Spirit to let you know when/how to speak to this person. Ask Him to give you a quiet heart to hear when this happens.

THOUGHTS

This space is here for you to jot down some thoughts, write out a prayer, draw a picture, or do whatever you want to help you remember your 10-minute moment.

ROMANS
12:1-2

Most of the New Testament (everything from Matthew on) was written by a guy named Paul. Years before he wrote most of these books, Paul actually was persecuting followers of Jesus, throwing them in jail, even having them killed. But then one day, Jesus appeared to him in a vision. This vision changed Paul's life, and after that Paul committed his life to telling others about Jesus. Most of Paul's books in the Bible are letters he wrote to different churches, helping them know how to live the Christian life as God wanted. That's where today's passage comes from – Paul's letter to the church in Rome.

TWO MINUTES

Read the passage several times (as many times as you can in 2 minutes).

Romans 12:1-2 (NLT)
¹And so, dear brothers and sisters, I plead with you to give your bodies to God because of all he has done for you. Let them be a living and holy sacrifice—the kind he will find acceptable. This is truly the way to worship him. ²Don't copy the behavior and customs of this world, but let God transform you into a new person by changing the way you think. Then you will learn to know God's will for you, which is good and pleasing and perfect.

5 MINUTES

Think about the following questions and how they might apply to your life.

- In v. 2 it says to think like God, not like the world. What are some things "the world" (friends at school, TV, movies, etc.) thinks that are different from how Jesus thinks?
- In v. 1 it says to be a "living sacrifice." What do you think of when you hear the word "sacrifice"? What do you think it means to be a "living sacrifice?"
- What does it mean to "give your bodies to God"? What are some ways you could do that?

3 MINUTES

Spend 3 minutes talking to God. Here are some things to talk to Him about today.
- Worship is anytime we put God's way before our way. Ask God to help you honor Him today through how you use your body (how you dress, the words you say, the things you look at, etc.).
- God doesn't just want us to "obey the rules," He wants us to learn how to always say "God, what do you want me to do," believing that He loves us and wants what's best for us. Ask God to help you be a "living sacrifice" today (this means to give Him your choices and decisions – to sacrifice your right to do what you want).

THOUGHTS

This space is here for you to jot down some thoughts, write out a prayer, draw a picture, or do whatever you want to help you remember your 10-minute moment.

COLOSSIANS
3:1-3

A big idea in Paul's writings is an idea that sounds kind of creepy – "dying with Christ." But it's not as weird as it sounds. Paul says that whenever we give our lives to Jesus, the old part of us (the part that was disobedient and separated from God) dies. The new us – the new creation as Paul puts it – is alive and free to follow Jesus! That's what Paul is getting at in this verse:

2 MINUTES

Read the passage several times (as many times as you can in 2 minutes).

Colossians 3:1-3 (NLT)

1Since you have been raised to new life with Christ, set your sights on the realities of heaven, where Christ sits in the place of honor at God's right hand. 2Think about the things of heaven, not the things of earth. 3For you died to this life, and your real life is hidden with Christ in God.

5 MINUTES

Think about the following questions and how they might apply to your life.

- What do you think it means to "think about the things of heaven, not the things of earth"? Is Paul saying "dream about angels and harps and fluffy clouds" (which isn't what heaven's like anyway!)? Is that what it means to think about heaven, or is there more to it?

- How does it make you feel to think that the "old you" – the part that couldn't stop sinning – is dead? If it's true that we're a "new creation" then why do you think we still sin so much?

Here's the truth – you ARE a new creation. Because the power of the Holy Spirit is at work in your life, you are free from sin. But we have all kinds of bad habits we've built up here on earth. We've learned to lie and be jealous and afraid and insecure. Jesus wants to teach us to learn NEW habits. He wants you to imagine a life where you aren't afraid of what other people thought because you know Jesus loves you. He wants you to see other people the way HE does – as valuable and beautiful and worth being kind to.

This is part of what it means to "think about the things of heaven" – it means to focus on how God intended things to be instead of constantly filling our minds with the junk of how things are.

3 MINUTES

Spend 3 minutes talking to God. Here are some things to talk to Him about today.
- Ask God to give you a desire to spend more and more time with Him. Ask Him to change the way you think, so that you care about what He cares about.
- Pray for a family member or a friend who you know needs prayer. Ask God to show you how you can encourage that person this week.
- Talk to God about what's going on in your life, including any needs you might have coming up.

THOUGHTS

This space is here for you to jot down some thoughts, write out a prayer, draw a picture, or do whatever you want to help you remember your 10-minute moment.

Back in Genesis it said that God created everything, and that it was perfect. But then Adam and Eve sinned, and things got messed up. For thousands of years after that, God had a plan to come down as a man, die and rise again, and free anyone who believed from the separation that had occurred between man and God. But right now, even for those of us who believe, there's still a sort of separation, right? Yes, the Holy Spirit lives with us, but when can we see God face to face? When can we actually live in a world that was how it was supposed to be, with no pain or fighting or death? Is that part of God's plan?

2 MINUTES

Read the passage several times (as many times as you can in 2 minutes).

Revelation 21:1-5 (NLT)
1Then I saw a new heaven and a new earth, for the old heaven and the old earth had disappeared. And the sea was also gone. 2And I saw the holy city, the new Jerusalem, coming down from God out of heaven like a bride beautifully dressed for her husband.

3I heard a loud shout from the throne, saying, "Look, God's home is now among his people! He will live with them, and they will be his people. God himself will be with them. 4He will wipe every tear from their eyes, and there will be no more death or sorrow or crying or pain. All these things are gone forever."

5And the one sitting on the throne said, "Look, I am making everything new!" And then he said to me, "Write this down, for what I tell you is trustworthy and true."

5 MINUTES

Think about the following questions and how they might apply to your life.

- In v. 3 it says "God's home is now among His people." What do you think that means? How is that different than now?
- What does God say He'll do in v. 4?
- Is it easy or hard for you to live your life, remembering that one day Jesus is going to come back?
- If you COULD remember that all the time, how would that change how you lived now?

Truth is, God STILL has a plan for the world. He wants as many people to believe in Him so that when He comes back He can live with them. (People who don't accept God now can't be in His presence when they die or He returns. Being completely separated from God's presence is what hell is). His plan for your life is that you would use all your gifts, abilities, and relationships for Him, and to tell other people about Him. He wants you to be fully alive – the best that you can possibly be. We're going to struggle with being that person – God knows that and loves us anyway. The good news is that one day, it won't be hard anymore to love God and obey. One day we'll live in a perfect world and be in a perfect relationship with Him. Until then, we spend every day learning to love Him more. THAT is God's plan for our life.

THREE MINUTES

Spend 3 minutes talking to God. Here are some things to talk to Him about today.

- The Bible says that when we get to heaven we'll see Jesus. If this is exciting to you, tell Jesus you can't wait to see Him. If this seems weird to you, that's okay. Ask Jesus to help you get excited about that day.
- Thank God for inviting you into His plan. Ask Him to help you trust that He will always take care of you.
- Spend time praying for people around you who need help. Ask God to show you how you can help them.

TH●UGHTS

This space is here for you to jot down some thoughts, write out a prayer, draw a picture, or do whatever you want to help you remember your 10-minute moment.